DAILY MOTIVATION

DO THIS EVERYDAY

Your Life Begins With The First Decision You Make Every Morning

Winston Barber

Table of Contents

Chapter 1: Believe In Yourself 6
Chapter 2: Being Mentally Strong 8
Chapter 3: Be Inspired to Create 10
Chapter 4: Be Motivated by Challenge 12
Chapter 5: To Make Big Gains, Avoid Tiny Losses 15
Chapter 6: Stop Being a Slave To Old Beliefs 18
Chapter 7: Make Your Life Better By Saying "Thank You" 21
Chapter 8: How To Start Working Immediately 24
Chapter 9: Happy People Stay Greatful 28
Chapter 10: Going Through Tough Times Is Part of The Journey 31
Chapter 11: Get Rid of Worry and Focus On The Work 34
Chapter 12: Get Motivated Even When You Don't Feel Like IT 38
Chapter 13: Don't Wait Another Second To Live You Dreams 41
Chapter 14: Do the Painful Things First 45
Chapter 15: Distraction Is Robbing You 47
Chapter 16: Discomfort Is Temporary 50
Chapter 17: Develop Mental Toughness In The Face of Adversity 53
Chapter 18: Dealing With Addiction To Technology 56
Chapter 19: Creating Successful Habits 60
Chapter 20: Consistency 65
Chapter 21: Block Out The Critics and Detractors 68
Chapter 22: Start Each Day Stress-Free 71
Chapter 23: Stop Hitting That Snooze Button 74
Chapter 24: Crucial Life Skills To Have 76
Chapter 25: Steps to Identify Your Personal Core Values 80
Chapter 26: Steps To Get Out of Your Comfort Zone 85
Chapter 27: Schedule Your Motivation 91
Chapter 28: Ways To Focus on Creating Positive Actions 94

Chapter 29: Ways To Be Inspired..98
Chapter 30: How You're Demotivated by Burnout 102
Chapter 31: Ways To Master Your Next Move.....................................105

Chapter 1:

Believe in Yourself

Listen up. I want to tell you a story. This story is about a boy. A boy who became a man, despite all odds. You see, when he was a child, he didn't have a lot going for him. The smallest and weakest in his class, he had to struggle every day just to keep up with his peers. Every minute of every hour was a fight against an opponent bigger and stronger than he was - and every day he was knocked down. Beaten. Defeated. But... despite that... despite everything that was going against him... this small, weak boy had one thing that separated him from hundreds of millions of people in this world. A differentiating factor that made a difference in the matter of what makes a winner in this world of losers. You see this boy believed in himself. No matter the odds, he believed fundamentally that he had the power to overcome anything that got in his way! It didn't matter how many times he was knocked down, he got RIGHT BACK UP!

Now it wasn't easy. It hurt like hell. Every time he failed was another reminder of how far behind he was. A reminder of the nearly insurmountable gap between him and everyone else and lurking behind that reminder was the temptation, the suggestion to just give up. Throw in the towel. Surrender the win. Yet believe me when I tell you that no matter HOW tough things got, no matter HOW much he wanted to give in, a small voice in his heart keep saying... not today... just once more... I know it hurts but I can try again... Just. Once. More.

You see more than anything in this world HE KNEW that deep inside him was a greatness just WAITING to be tapped into! A power that most people would never see, but not him. It didn't matter what the world threw at him, because he'd be damned if he let his potential die alongside him. And all it took? All it required to unlock the chasm of greatness inside was a moment to realise the lies the world tried to tell him. In less than a second he recognised the light inside that would ignite a spark of success to address the ones who didn't believe that he could do it. The ones who told him to give up! Get out! Go home and roam the streets where failure meets those who weren't born to sit at the seat at the top!

Yet what they didn't know is that being born weak didn't matter any longer 'cause in his fight to succeed he became stronger. Rising up to the heights beyond, he WOULD NOT GIVE UP till he forged a bond within his heart that ensured NO MATTER THE ODDS, no matter what anyone said about him, no matter what the world told him, he had something that NO ONE could take away from him. A power so strong it transformed this boy into a man. A loser into a winner. A failure into a success. That, is the power of self-belief...

Chapter 2:

Being Mentally Strong

Have you ever wondered why your performance in practice versus an actual test is like night and day? Or how you are able to perform so well in a mock situation but just crumble when it comes game time?

It all boils down to our mental strength.

The greatest players in sports all have one thing in common, incredibly strong beliefs in themselves that they can win no matter how difficult the circumstance. Where rivals that have the same playing ability may challenge them, they will always prevail because they know their self-worth and they never once doubt that they will lose even when facing immense external or internal pressure.

Most of us are used to facing pressure from external sources. Whether it be from people around us, online haters, or whoever they may be, that can take a toll on our ability to perform. But the greatest threat is not from those areas... it is from within. The voices in our head telling us that we are not going to win this match, that we are not going to well in this performance, that we should just give up because we are already losing by that much.

It is only when we can crush these voices that we can truly outperform our wildest abilities. Mental strength is something that we can all acquire. We just have to find a way to block out all the negativity and replace them with voices that are encouraging. to believe in ourselves that we can and will overcome any situation that life throws at us.

The next time you notice that doubts start creeping in, you need to snap yourself out of it as quickly as you can, 5 4 3 2 1. Focus on the next point, focus on the next game, focus on the next speech. Don't give yourself the time to think about what went wrong the last time. You are only as good as your present performance, not your past.

I believe that you will achieve wonderful things in life you are able to crush those negative thoughts and enhance your mental strength.

Chapter 3:

Be Inspired to Create

Some of you will look in the mirror today and think that you are weird. You will see that you are different to other people. That you are quirky or odd. But I want to encourage you. Not only is your uniqueness something that you should embrace but it is perhaps your greatest asset. The wonderful thing about people being different is that they think a little differently, see the world from a slightly different perspective. The combination of the various bits of knowledge that they have fit together in different ways.

When you speak you are most likely not conscious of your accent. Maybe if you live in a foreign country you are hyper aware of it. But how many of you know that your mind has an accent too. It has an accent that is formed from your experiences. Your experiences with pain. Your experiences with joy. Your experiences with success, failure and even your experiences with the everyday mundane. Not only that but the accent of your mind constantly evolves.

Why does that matter?

Because it is that accent which enables you to innovate. When you speak a foreign word, it takes on a new form in your accent – sometimes it may even be a sound that has never been uttered with that tone and inflection.

It is completely original not because of the form of the word but because of the accent that informs the way the word comes out.

The same is true of your mind. You can speak the same ideas, study the same fields, even research the exact same thing and still end up with different outcomes. How? Because your outcomes are being informed by your experiences. Your ideas are your present thoughts running rampant through familiar thought patterns. They are tailored towards a particular style. For some of you it is like your mind rolls the r's in your ideas. It adds a certain *je ne sais quoi* to your ideas. To others your accent is thick and mutes the aesthetic nuances of ideas – manifesting in wonders of logic and mechanics.

Whatever it may be, I encourage you to embrace the accent of your mind. Actually, I demand you to. It is time that you stopped denying the world of your contribution to it. It's time that you got inspired to create. It is time that you allowed ideas to implode within the realm of your consciousness and innovations to pour out of it. Whether you find your language in art, dance, engineering, or politics. If you have a niche area of knowledge or see a pattern from a unique combination of information then it is about time you harnessed that and rode the creation train to wherever it may take you. I can promise you that you will never look back. We tend to regret the things we did not do, not the things that we did.

Listen closely and hear the accentuation of your thoughts. Then speak their creative ingenuity into being.

Create something that only you can.

Chapter 4:

Be Motivated by Challenge

You have an easy life and a continuous stream of income, you are lucky! You have everything you and your children need, you are lucky! You have your whole future planned ahead of you and nothing seems to go in the other direction yet, you are lucky!

But how far do you think this can go? What surety can you give yourself that all will go well from the start to the very end?

Life will always have a hurdle, a hardship, a challenge, right there when you feel most satisfied. What will you do then?

Will you give up and look for an escape? Will you seek guidance? Or will you just give up and go down a dark place because you never thought something like this could happen to you?

Life is full of endless possibilities and an endless parade of challenges that make life no walk in the park.

You are different from any other human being in at least one attribute. But your life isn't much different than most people's. You may be less fortunate or you may be the luckiest, but you must not back down when life strikes you.

This world is a cruel place and a harsh terrain. But that doesn't mean you should give up whenever you get hit in the back. That doesn't mean you don't catch what the world throws at you.

Do you know what you should do? Look around and observe for examples. Examples of people who have had the same experiences as you had and what good or bad things did they do? You will find people on both extremes.

You will find people who didn't have the courage or guts to stand up to the challenge and people who didn't have the time to give up but to keep pushing harder and harder, just to get better at what they failed the last time.

The challenges of life can never cross your limits because the limits of a human being are practically infinite. But what feels like a heavy load, is just a shadow of your inner fear dictating you to give up.

But you can't give up, right? Because you already have what you need to overcome this challenge too. You just haven't looked into your backpack of skills yet!

If you are struggling at college, go out there and prove everyone in their wrong. Try to get better grades by putting in more hours little by little.

If people take you as a non-social person, try to talk to at least one new person each day.

If you aren't getting good at a sport, get tutorials and try to replicate the professionals step by step and put in all your effort and time if you truly care for the challenge at hand.

The motivation you need is in the challenge itself. You just need to realize the true gains you want from each stone in your path and you will find treasures under every stone.

Chapter 5:

To Make Big Gains, Avoid Tiny Losses

Life is a process of adding and subtracting. We add the things that make us better and make life easier. We put aside the things that prove to be a pebble in the shoe.

There is a flaw in human effort and our concept for success. We think that we can achieve more if we focus harder on getting better. We think that if we are not getting worse, we are on the right track. But I can assure you, we are heavily mistaken.

The more we focus on bigger gains, the more we overlook the small things we stop caring about. We give up on relations, hobbies, ethics, love, and the million other losses that we don't measure on the same scale.

We can achieve the same amount of things, the same scale of success, and still, be the better person that we want to be. But we don't need to not work on the smaller details of this successful journey.

Let's say you have achieved it all and now you look back a decade or two. Do you think you won't regret the things that could have been saved in this whole process? But you chose not to or didn't care enough for them, and now you are rich in the pocket but poor in every other sense.

They say money can buy you anything, but it can never buy you happiness. You can have all the money in the world but you can't make sure if you won't ever have any regret.

We all are a creator. We make things, sometimes for ourselves and sometimes for people around us. Sometimes we make things better for us that then prove to be good for someone else as well. But also do things in a way that doesn't affect anyone else in a bad way. At least not deliberately.

Bad things happen, but most of the time we are the reason for them to happen in the first place. We are so devoted to the greater good that we neglect the small things we lose in the process.

Check it with yourself, if you are so devoted to being a better person than you were yesterday, and you have achieved more than yesterday. Then why do you still repeat the small mistakes and take the small losses?

You have to understand the concept of losses over gains. If you invest some money into something, and you are at a small loss every other day, then you can't justify the big profits you might gain some days later.

It is the constant concern to keep away from the small misfortunes or mistakes that might leave you into yet another breakdown. If you truly want to be a free and successful person, you need to have confidence in whatever you do will certainly give you more and more and it won't come at the cost of a single thing.

Take the mantra, reduce your losses and your gains will gain volumes in no time.

Chapter 6:

Stop Being a Slave To Old Beliefs

Life has a beginning for everyone. Everyone has a different life. Everyone has a different belief. Everyone has different brains and different observations. You are that everyone. You are different in every aspect possible except the fact that you are only human life to a billion others.

We humans, as a species have lived history through a certain set of rules. Modern and civilized cultures live with some social decorum and follow some societal beliefs and rituals. But who imposed these laws on us?

Who made these rituals so important for everyone, as if we cannot survive without them? There is no justification for most of these beliefs that are still being practiced to date.

Humans have also the same ways of adapting to thins like other animals. They tend to repeat things to perfect or learn them.

We have practiced so many pointless beliefs and conditions for so long that we are unwilling and unable to even try to think aside them.

We are so scared to look around these beliefs and shake things up a bit to create newer and better outcomes for us and others. But we still feel liable and a slave to this tendency to follow whatever is being imposed on us. No!

You are a free soul. You were born a free soul. You were given a unique mind and you should act like you still have one. You can think of bigger and better ways to make your life easier and more meaningful.

Look at a bird. They start taking lessons from other birds, but when they are finally in the air for the first time, they are now free to do anything they can ever wish to do.

You are also a free bird. You have everything you want to create new beliefs of your own where you don't have to justify or answer to anyone because now you have a person to fall back on. And that person is You!

What if you started a cult today, and someone came and asked you to justify it. Do you think you owe that person an answer? I don't think so!

Because you are a free individual who can anything he or she wants, only if it doesn't hurt anyone else around you.

You started your life alone and you will die alone. So why not live it alone too. I am not saying to give up on all relations. But you should make up your own beliefs if you are not OK with the previous ones.

Don't argue! You cannot force your opinion on anyone else, just like you are not obligated to follow anyone else's.

So from this day in your life. Make a vow to yourself, that you will take every day of your life as if it were a new life and you will discover newer things this time. This will help you find a newer purpose and will eventually create a new ambition for others to follow.

Chapter 7:

Make Your Life Better By Saying 'Thank You'

We are an ungrateful species. We are not grateful enough for what we have on our plates or for what someone else does for it. Even if we are on the receiving end of it, we don't appreciate it much.

We think that the word 'Thank you should be reserved for a very special moment. We treat it as if it is a very posh word and can't be used in many instances. But the reality is that we are not grateful enough to have the courage to thank more than we are doing right now.

You are not losing anything and it certainly doesn't affect your image in others' eyes. It surely helps to get things done more easily and quickly if you were to thank more often. It would help you get a better place in others' judgment of you and it would help you fit in with anyone.

Let's say you were to receive congrats for any of your achievements from any of your colleagues. Would it be rude if you weren't to return the compliment with a simple 'Thank You'?

Wouldn't you be called an egotistical person for not even appreciating the other with a simple compliment?

What if you were to say 'Thank You' for even the smallest of virtues happening to you? You would be praised for your gratitude towards others and you would be celebrated even more for even your smallest achievements.

You not only have to thank the people around you, but you should also thank god or your luck or your life for every moment that led you to this day.

Thank you for the hard times that made you appreciate the good times. Thank you for the lessons that you needed for you personal development. Thank you for a healthy life. Thank you for all the energies that drive me. Thank you for the drive. Thank you for the confidence. Thank you for my spirit. Thank you for the courage to keep me going through the hard times. Thank you for everything that we take for granted.

You should thank the people in your life that make your life worth living for. Thank them more than often because they have done a lot for you and also thank them for everything they will do for you in the future.

It won't hurt you to be grateful to others and it won't make anyone want you less. It will only increase your importance in others' life and them wanting to do more for you.

Take some time out of your life every day and just run your whole day like a flashback. Concentrate on the moments of respect and kindness that you received from anyone. Take some time out the next day and just go and thank them all. You would be surprised by what you receive from them, and what it makes you feel for yourself. Your trust in humanity will be immortal with this simple habit!

Chapter 8:

How To Start Working Immediately

"There is only one way for me to motivate myself to work hard: I don't think about it as hard work. I think about it as part of making myself into who I want to be. Once I've chosen to do something, I try not to think so much about how difficult or frustrating or impossible that might be; I just think about how good it must feel to be that or how proud I might be to have done that. Make hard look easy." - Marie Stein.

Motivation is somewhat elusive. Some days you feel it naturally, other days you don't, no matter how hard you try. You stare at your laptop screen or your essay at the desk, willing yourself to type or write; instead, you find yourself simply going through the motions, not caring about the work that you're producing. You're totally uninspired, and you don't know how to make yourself feel otherwise. You find yourself being dissatisfied, discouraged, frustrated, or disappointed to get your hands on those long-awaited tasks. While hoping for things to change and make our lives better overnight magically, we waste so much of our precious time. Sorry to burst your bubble, but things just don't happen like that. You have to push yourself off that couch, turn off the phone, switch off Netflix and make it happen. There's no need to seek anyone's permission or blessings to start your work.

The world doesn't care about how tired you are. Or, if you're feeling depressed or anxious, stop feeling sorry for yourself while you're at it. It doesn't matter one bit. We all face obstacles and challenges and struggles throughout our days, but how we deal with those obstacles and difficulties defines us and our successes in life. As James Clear once said, "Professionals stick to the schedule, amateurs let life get in the way. Professionals know what is important to them and work towards it with purpose; amateurs get pulled off course by the urgencies of life."

Take a deep breath. Brew in your favorite coffee. Eat something healthy. Take a shower, take a walk, talk to someone who lifts your energy, turn off your socials, and when you're done with all of them, set your mind straight and start working immediately. Think about the knowledge, the skill, the experience that you'll gain from working. Procrastination might feel good but imagine how amazing it will feel when you'll finally get your tasks, your work done. Don't leave anything for tomorrow. Start doing it today. We don't know what tomorrow might bring for us. If we will be able even to wake up and breathe. We don't know it for sure. So, start hustling today. You just need that activation energy to start your chain of events.

Start scheduling your work on your calendar and actually follow it. We may feel like we have plenty of time to get things done. Hence, we tend to ignore our work and take it easy. But to tell you the truth, time flickers by in seconds. Before you know it, you're already a week behind your deadline, and you still haven't started working yet. Keep reminding yourself as to why you need to do this work done. Define your goals and get them into action. Create a clear and compelling vision of your work. You only achieve what you see. Break your work into small, manageable tasks so you stay motivated throughout your work procedure. Get yourself organized. Unclutter your mind. Starve your distractions. Create that perfect environment so you can keep up with your work until you're done. Please choose to be successful and then stick to it.

You may feel like you're fatigued, or your mind will stop producing ideas and creativity after a while. But that's completely fine. Take a break. Set a timer for five minutes. Force yourself to work on the thing for five minutes, and after those five minutes, it won't feel too bad to keep going. Make a habit of doing the small tasks first, so they get out of the way, and you can harness your energy to tackle the more significant projects.

Reward yourself every time you complete your work. This will boost your confidence and will give you the strength to continue with your remaining tasks. Don't let your personal and professional responsibilities overwhelm you. Help yourself stay focused by keeping in mind that you're accountable for your own actions. Brian Roemmele, the Quora user, encourages people to own every moment, "You are in full control of this power. In your hands, you can build the tallest building and, in your hands, you can destroy the tallest buildings."

Start surrounding yourself with people who are an optimist and works hard. The saying goes, you're the average of the five people you hang out with the most. So, make sure you surround yourself with people who push you to succeed.

No matter how uninspired or de-motivating it may seem, you have to take that first step and start working. Whether it's a skill that you're learning, a language that you want to know, a dance step that you wish to perfect, a business idea that you want to implement, an instrument that you want to master, or simply doing the work for anyone else, you should do it immediately. Don't wait for the next minute, the next hour, the next day, or the following week; start doing your stuff. No one else is going to do your work for you, nor it's going to be completed by itself. Only you have the power to get on with it and get it done. Get your weak spots fixed. In the end, celebrate your achievements whether it's small or big. Imagine the relief of not having that task up on your plate anymore. Visualize yourself succeeding. It can help you stay to stay focused and motivated and get your work done. Even the worst tasks won't feel painful, but instead, they'll feel like a part of achieving something big.

Remember, motivation starts within. Find it, keep it and make it work wonders for you.

Chapter 9:

Happy People Stay Grateful For Everything They Have

A lot of us will have different answers to this simple question, "what are you grateful for today?" It could differ from as simple as getting out of bed to achieving that huge task you had your mind on for a while. Gratitude is the emotion we feel when we tend to notice and appreciate the good things that have come into our lives. Some people feel grateful for even the tiniest things, while others don't even if they achieve more than they have wished for. Most of the time, people who will be thankful still feel negative emotions, but they tend to shift their focus from all the bad things in their lives to the good ones.

Research has shown that teenagers and adults who feel more grateful than others are also happier, get better grades, have better friends, get more opportunities, have fewer illnesses and pain, have more energy, and tend to sleep better. The link of practicing gratitude to achieve happiness is through a path that we commonly call the "cognitive pathway." The words "cognitive" and "cognition" are used by scientists to talk about thinking; if we don't think about the good things in our life, we would not feel grateful.

Most situations that happen in our lives are neither all good nor all bad. It is on us how we trick our minds and interpret the effect of the situation on our lives. One of the thinking habits is called a "positive interpretation bias," which means that we are most likely to interpret a neutral or negative situation positively. On the contrary, some people tend to ignore all the positive aspects of their problems and finds excuses and reasons to focus more on the negativity.

Studies also show that people who practice gratitude remember more good memories than bad ones. A more grateful person tends to encode more positive memories and keeps out the negative ones. They are also tended to be healthier and are sick less often. This is because they worry less about all the wrong things and focus more on the positive stuff they had achieved throughout the days. They keep their negative emotions to a minimum. A study showed that people who felt more grateful also had increased brain activity essential for both emotional and cognitive processes.

Happiness and gratitude go hand in hand and can be practiced in a lot of different ways. One way is to write a list of all the good things that have happened to you every day and go through it before you sleep. Another way is to send some love to your close ones, thanking and appreciating all that they have done for you. While it is essential to practice gratitude every day, it is also important to know that the bad things shouldn't be ignored. In fact, the real test of gratitude is how we act on the situations when they don't go as per our plans. We don't always need to be happy to be grateful, but gratitude indeed leads to greater happiness.

Chapter 10:

Going Through Tough Times Is Part of The Journey

For someone going through tough times, for someone going through the same hardships, again and again, every day, you are trying but not getting used to all this.

Things never seem to get better and you don't think you are just right there to get a hold of things. You think you will get them this time, but they always seem to be going a new way that you never planned.

It's alright! You are not the first one to think about things this way are you certainly won't be the last one.

You are not the first person to think that you will have different achievements this time. You are not the first person to think that you will achieve bigger goals this year. You are not the first person to fail at every corner after all that determination and grit.

Life always kicks us on the blindside, and most of us know what it feels like. But not all of us want to stay in the bed all day and feel sorry for ourselves for what happened before.

People always find a way to cope with the tragedies of life. And these people know the true purpose of life. They know the true definition of life. Wanna know what that is? It's the hard times that make you a harder more precious gem.

You can never possibly understand why it is happening to you because it is what it is and you can never set your back to reality.
The reality is that no one has ever lived a reasonable life without facing the hard times. And only the people who smiled back at these hard times had a happy ending in the end.

The only thing that makes us go through life with a smile in the hope of getting a big reward at the end of it all. Our lives aren't judged on the number of success stories we write, but with the techniques, we adapt to tackle the moments when life pushes us against a wall.

It won't always be your fault but it might be your luck trying to test your limits. So why don't you show it?

Things will always go wrong in your life but that doesn't make it justifiable to put everything aside and start mourning and regretting your every mistake and every flaw. But it's time to start removing those flaws to minimize your mistakes and trying to be a perfect individual.

This is the journey to perfection that makes going through hard times justifiable. Because every stone that your pick and set aside is another hurdle being cleared for an easier road to the top.

What happens to you in life is just a glimpse of the reality, but what you do about those things in life is what living this life is actually about.

Always remember, you and your life are always like a plane. You both fly against the winds but never along it.

Chapter 11:

Get Rid of Worry and Focus On The Work

Worry is the active process of bringing one's fears into reality.

Worrying about problems halts productivity by taking your mind off the work in hand.

If you're not careful, a chronic state of worrying can lead you down a dark path that you might find hard to get out of.

Always focus on the required work and required action towards your dream.

Anything could happen, good or bad,

but if you remain focused and do the work despite the problems,

you will through with persistence and succeed.

Always keep your mind on the goal,

your eyes on the prize.

Have an unwavering faith in your abilities no matter what.

Plan for the obvious obstacles that could stand in your way,

but never worry about them until you have to face them.

Tackle it with confidence as they come and move forward with pride.

Problems are bound to arise.

Respond to them necessarily along the way if they actually happen.

After all, most worries never make it into reality.

Instead focus on what could go right.

Focus on how you can create an environment that will improve your chances of success.

You have the power over your own life and direction.

As children we dreamed big.

We didn't think about all the things that could go wrong.

As children we only saw the possibilities.

We were persistent in getting what we wanted no matter the cost.

As adults we need to be reminded of that child-like faith.

To crush worry as if it were never there.

To only focus on the possibilities.

You cannot be positive and negative at the same time.

You cannot be worrying and hopeful of the future.

You cannot visualize your perfect life while worrying about everything that could go wrong.

Choose one.

Stick to it.

Choose to concentrate on the work.

The result will take care of your worries.

Catch yourself when you feel yourself beginning to worry about things.

Instead of dwelling on the problem, choose to double down on the action.
Stay focused and steadfast in the vision of your ultimate goal.

The work now that you must do is the steppingstones to your success.
The work now must have your immediate attention.
The work now requires you to cast worry aside in favour of concentration and focus.

How many steppingstones are you away?
What is next?
Push yourself every single day.
Because only you have the power to create your future.
If not, things will remain the same as they have always been.

Always have a clearly defined goal,
A strong measure of faith,
And an equally strong measure of persistence and grit.
These are the ingredients to creating the life you want.
A life of lasting happiness and success.

Take control instead of accepting things as they are.
Reject anything else that is not the goal that you've set for yourself.
Whatever goal you set, ten times it, and focus on it every day.
The focus will keep your mind on the work until you succeed.
There will be no time to worry when you are too busy taking constant action.

Always have the belief in your heart and soul that you will succeed.

Never let a grain of doubt cast a shadow in your eventual path to victory.

Focus is key to all.

What you focus on, you will create.

Worrying is worse than useless,

it is DETRIMENTAL to your future.

Take control of your thoughts.

When worry pops it's ugly head, force it out with a positive thought of your future.

Don't let the negative illusions of worry live rent-free in your mind.

You are in control here.

Of what you watch,

What you read,

What you listen too

And what you think.

What you think of consistently will become.

Focus on what you want, and how to get there is crucial for lasting happiness and success.

Chapter 12:

Get Motivated Even When You Don't Feel Like It

Have you ever heard of the LOCUS Rule? If you haven't, let me explain it to you. The Locus of control is the aspect of your life in which you come to realize the degree to which you believe you have control over your life and the things revolving around it.

Let's simplify it with an example. Let's say you are presented with a situation where you have to solve a puzzle. When you attempt it, luckily you solve it in record time. Someone comes to you and says that you were able to do it because you are smart.

The next time you are presented with a relatively simpler problem, you spend much more time on it and might not be able to solve some hard ones at all. So you feel demotivated and you don't want to do any more puzzles.

But if you were to spend a considerable time solving the original puzzle while doing calculations and taking educational guesses and thinking a lot. Someone would have pointed out that you are a hard worker, so good Job!

So the next time you would feel more motivated to do any similar job and you might be able to perform better in the next one's.

The first case was determined by an external, unprecedented, immeasurable, God-gifted feat. If at any time, you cannot get something done, you would think that you don't have it in you anymore and you are just a piece of sheer luck.

But if you know for sure that you can achieve absolutely anything, just as you keep doing what you do best, and that being your hard work. Then everything seems achievable, and everything seems easy no matter how long it gets.

Life is a balloon stretched over this rule. Life always presents us with opportunities, but we miss out on most. We miss out because we have this fear of non-confidence within us. We fear the unknown and so we get stuck in the same old rut of depression, anxiety, and fear.

All these things have a simple initiative for a solution.

You need to be transparent with yourself. You need to prove your strengths and strategies to yourself. And you have to tell it to yourself that you only need a little willpower to always keep one little straw to stick to, for when every support seems to turn to dust.

Look around you. You are still a lot better than the majority. You still have a brain to keep you on your ability to self-analyze.

Think about it. You failed today, but you had some success some time ago. So if you can spend some time feeling sorry for yourself, you can spend the same time trying to put your mind, heart, and body to get up one more time and try one more time.

You might fail again and again and again but remember that life is not based on one moment of luck. Life is a campaign of hard work followed by dedication and motivation.

Chapter 13:

Don't Wait Another Second To Live Your Dreams

We often think we must be ready to act, but the truth is we will never be ready while we wait.

We only become ready by walking the path, and battles are seldom won in ideal circumstances.

Money is not the real currency in life, the real currency is time and every second we wait is a second, we waste.

Your biggest motivator is the ticking clock and the impending reality that one day it will be too late.

Your biggest fear is getting to 80 and realizing you haven't lived, that you haven't done what you wanted in life because of fear.

True regret is a medicine none of us want to taste.

We must decide what we really want, set the bar high, go after it now and accept nothing less.

You deserve respect, but you will live what you expect, this life will pay you any price but it's up to you what you accept.

You must act now from where we are with what we have, right now, not tomorrow or next week, right now.

Take the first step, make the draft plan.

Find out what knowledge you need to make this dream a reality.

Taking action now towards the goal in mind is crucial, if we wait, we risk losing the drive to make things happen.

We can never be fully ready because we don't know what exactly is going to happen, a lot of it is learned along the way - especially if you're doing something brand new.

If not, reading what has been done before in your area will give you a good understanding of what might work.

Every second we spend thinking about, instead of acting towards our goal is wasted time.

You cannot afford to wait because if you do not act, someone else will, someone else could also be thinking what you're thinking and act first.

Those who wait for opportunity will wait in vain because opportunity must be created, first in the mind, then in the world.

We cannot see the vast opportunity that surrounds us unless we believe it is there, believe it is possible and act on that belief, at the time it arises.

The world is pliable, and opportunities do not wait for people to be ready. You must become ready on the road.

The obstacles you have to overcome on the move will mold you into the person you need to be to reach your biggest goals.

You must be patient, to be practitioners of who you believe you will be one day.

Getting into the mindset of whoever you want to be right now, because until you become that person in mind, you cannot in body.

As we start acting differently, different actions bring different results and if the new actions are positive and aimed at a certain goal, just like magic the world begins to transform for you, towards the life you wanted.

The leap of faith is acting now, feeling unready aiming for something that may seem unrealistic, but this is an essential leap and test to be overcome. As the days go on with the goal in mind, it will seem to become more likely, and you will feel more ready until it feels definite.

All things are possible but there will be required ingredients to your success you might not know yet, so the first step is to gain the knowledge required.

Once you begin to learn that knowledge you are on the road to your goal. Organization and optimization of your time will make it easier to be efficient.

If time is the real currency, are you getting good value for what you spend your time doing?

If not, is it not time you used some of your seconds working towards something phenomenal?

You only have so many, and it is losing value every day as we age, think about it.

We must create a sense of urgency because it is urgent if you want to succeed in an ever-changing world.

If we wait our ideas, products and services may become irrelevant because new technology and innovation is always changing.

Our ideas are only viable when they come,

Strike while the iron is hot is good advice,

When the ambition and goal is strongest and clearest.

Clarity is essential when pursuing dreams and goals, every detail of your dream should be clear in your mind down to the sights, colours and smells.

When we think about our goal, we should feel it as if it's already here, and start acting like it is.

Dress talk and walk as if you are that person now.

Whatever our current circumstances everyone has the ability to build in their minds, set the goal then determine the first step.

If your circumstances are bad there are more steps, but there are steps.

Start from step one and walk in confidence always keeping the big dream in mind knowing that this can happen for you.

We have a waking mind and a subconscious mind.

The subconscious knows things we don't, it is responsible for our gut instinct, which always seems to be right so follow that.

Everyday listening to that voice, keeping a clear vision of your goal in your mind and confidently taking action towards it.

It's possible for you if you act,

But time is ticking.

Chapter 14:

Do The Painful Things First

There are a lot of secret recipes to be happier; one of them is seek what's painful first. Sure, this may sound a little ironic, but you will be surprised to know that all scientific research is behind this. Behavioral scientists discovered that one of the most effective ways to create an enjoyable experience is to stack the painful parts of the experience early in the process. For example, if you're a doctor, a lawyer, accountant, etc., it's better to break bad news first and then finish with the good news. This will give the clients a more satisfying experience since you start poorly then end on a solid note instead of starting well and ending badly.

There's a couple of crucial reasons why we should do the painful things first. We know that we have limited willpower during the day, and we also know that the most painful activities or tasks are sometimes the most difficult ones. So if we complete the things we find the most difficult first, we'll be exerting less energy on less complicated activities for the rest of the day. Scientific studies show that our prefrontal cortex (creative part of the brain) is the most active the moment we wake up. At the same time, the analytical parts of our brain (the editing and proofreading parts) become more active as the day goes on.

Another reason to do the painful activities firsthand after you wake up is that you would be freed from all the distractions and tend to do these tasks more quickly. If you delay the complex tasks, it will only come back to bite you. Starting with only one task for a day can be enough, as it could lead you to achieve more of them as time goes by. Things like building a new business, losing weight, or learning a new skill require pain and slow work in the beginning to get momentum. But after some persistence, you will likely see your improvements. Behavioral psychology suggests that we're more likely to lead a happier life if we're making improvements over time. Anthony Robbins once said, "If you're not growing, you're dying."

Making slow but gradual improvements is where persistency comes in. It's going to be painful and frustrating initially, and you won't learn a new language in an instant, or your business won't thrive immediately. But when you decide to sacrifice your short-term pleasure for a future pay-off, you will get to enjoy the long-term benefits over a sustained period. Stop avoiding what's hard; embrace it for your long-term happiness.

Chapter 15:

Distraction Is Robbing You

Every second you spend doing something that is not moving you
towards your goal, you are robbing yourself of precious time.
Stop being distracted!

You have something you need to do,
but for some reason become distracted by
other less important tasks and procrastinate on the important stuff.
Most people do it,
whether it's notification s on your phone or chat with colleges,
mostly less than half the working day is productive.

Distraction can be avoided by having a schedule
which should include some down time to relax
or perhaps get some of them distractions out of the way,
but time limited.

As long as everything has its correct time in
your day you can keep distraction from stealing too much of your time.
When your mind is distracted it becomes nearly impossible to
concentrate on the necessary work at hand.

Always keep this question in mind:
"is what I am about to do moving me towards my goal?"
If not, is it necessary?
What could I do instead that will?

It's all about your 24 hours.
Your actions and the reactions to your actions from that day,
good or bad.
By keeping your mind focused on your schedule that
moves you towards your goal, you will become resilient to distraction.

Distraction is anything that is not on your schedule.
You may need to alter that depending on the importance of the intrusion.
Being successful means becoming single minded about your goal.
Those with faith do not need a plan b because they know plan A is the only way and they refuse to accept anything else.

Any time you spend contemplating failure will add to its chances of happening.
Why not focus on what will happen if you succeed instead?

Distraction from your vision of success is one of its biggest threats.
Blocking out distraction and keeping that vision clear is key.
Put that phone on flight mode and turn off the TV.
Focus on the truly important stuff.

If you don't do it, it will never get done.

The responsibility is all yours for everything in your life.

The responsibility is yours to block out the distractions and exercise your free-will over your thoughts and actions.

By taking responsibility and control you will become empowered.

Refuse to let anyone distract you when you're working.

Have a set time in your schedule to deal with stuff not on the schedule.

This will allow you time to deal with unexpected issues without stopping you doing the original work.

The reality is that we all only have so much time.

Do you really want to waste yours on distractions?

Do you want to not hit your target because of them?

Every time you stop for a notification on your phone you are losing time from your success.

Don't let distraction rob you of another second, minute, hour or day.

Days turn to months and months turn to years don't waste time on distractions and fears.

Chapter 16:

Discomfort Is Temporary

It's easy to get hopeless when things get a little overwhelming. It's easy to give up because you feel you don't have the strength or resources to continue. But where you stop is actually the start you have been looking for since the beginning.

Do you know what you should do when you are broken? You should relish it. You should use it. Because if you know you are broken, congratulations, you have found your limitations.

Now as you know what stopped you last time, you can work towards mending it. You can start to reinforce the breach and you should be able to fill in the cracks in no time.

Life never repeats everything. One day you feel the lowest and the next might bring you the most unpredictable gifts.

The world isn't all sunshine and rainbows. It is a very mean and nasty place to be in. But what can you do now when you are in it? Nothing? Never!

You have to endure the pain, the stress, the discomfort till you are comfortable with the discomfort. It doesn't make any sense, right? But listen to me.

You have a duty towards yourself. You have a duty towards your loved ones. You are expected to rise above all odds and be something no one has ever been before you. I know it might be a little too much to ask for, but, you have to understand your purpose.

Your purpose isn't just to sit on your back and the opportunities and blessings keep coming, knocking at your door, just so you can give up one more time and turn them down.

Things are too easy to reject and neglect but always get hard when you finally step up and go for them. But remember, every breathtaking view is from the top of a hill, but the trek to the top is always tiring. But when you get to the top, you find every cramp worth it.

If you are willing to put yourself through anything, discomfort and temporary small intervals of pain won't affect you in any way. As long as you believe that the experience will bring you to a new level.

If you are interested in the unknown, then you have to break barriers and cross your limits. Because every path that leads to success is full of them. But then and only then you will find yourself in a place where you are unbreakable.

You need to realize that your life is better than most people out there. You need to embrace the pain because all this is temporary. But when you are finally ready to embrace the pain, you are already on your way to a superior being.

Life is all about taking stands because we all get all kinds of blows. But we always need to dig in and keep fighting till we have found the gems or have found our last breath.

The pain and discomfort will subside one day, but if you quit, then you are already on the end of your rope.

Chapter 17:

Develop Mental Toughness In The Face of Adversity

The drawback of this technological revolution that we live in is that we have created a weaker generation, a weaker society. We need everything to be perfect, to be exactly the way we want it to be.

We can't bear a single change in our routines. We can't handle a single harmless task that might test us in any way possible. We can't forgive anyone's mistake, but we want all our blunders to be erased.

We can't handle the fact that life is always a step ahead of us. And if something bad happens, we try to mask it. We never try to actually deal with the problems, rather keep them at bay as long as we can.

We are so afraid of trying the do the things that would matter, but we become the wisest when we mock or advise someone else.

We are never truly prepared for the hard times. We are always in a constant fight with our own minds, neglecting reality and creating a false scenario where everything is alright. It is not Alright!

We are living in a time where everyone is in search of greatness. There are more and more people coming into this world every day and the competition is getting harder than it ever was. The day will come when we would have to fight for even the basic necessities of life.

The day might come when we will fail at almost everything we are doing right now. What will we do then?

Life gives us second chances, but those chances require us to be stronger. Those chances want us to first create some chances beforehand before we go forward with the grand scheme.

Chances present themselves to the people who are in the constant struggle to live every minute as if it were their last.

If someone was to ask you to join them for a morning run, you might be enthusiastic for one day. You will wake up at five in the morning, gear up, and go for 10 miles for the first day. On the second day, you will go for it again. A week later you will take a break for a day. A month later you might get a treadmill because you feel more comfortable running in your home rather than going out in the cold mornings. But eventually, you will stop doing it.

All of this is because you are not ready to get out of your comfort zone or not ready to commit for long enough to achieve what you started for.

Learn to say 'No' to 'No'. The day you start saying no to everything that will keep you in your warm cozy bed, is the day you will finally realize what you will achieve that day.

Life will always be hard on you, but you can join the league of successful beings if you stay true to your cause and keep pushing and digging till you finally find the gem of your choice.

Chapter 18:

Dealing With Addiction To Technology

Today we're going to talk about addiction to technology and media consumption. I think this is a topic that many of us can relate, even myself included. Am my goal for today is to try to help put forth a more sustainable and healthy habit for you to still enjoy technology while not being overwhelmed and overtaken by it completely.

So let's ask ourselves a simple question of why are we so hooked into using our devices so frequently and sparingly? I think for most of us, and this is my personal opinion, is that it offers us an escape, a distraction from our everyday tasks that we know we ought to do. To procrastinate just a little bit or to binge scroll on Instagram, Facebook, Snapchat, and what have you, to satisfy our need for media consumption.

We use technology as a tool a gateway into the world of digital media, and we get lost in it because companies try to feed us with posts and stuff that we like to keep us engaged and to keep us watching just a little while longer. And minutes can turn into hours, and before you know it, it is bedtime.

I want to argue that this addiction is not entirely your fault, but that these multi-billion-dollar mega companies are being fed so much data that they are able to manipulate us into consume their media. It is like how casinos use various tricks of flickering lights, and free drinks to keep you playing a little longer and to spend a little more of your attention and time. We unknowingly get subjected to these manipulative tactics, and we fall for it despite our best efforts to abstain from it.

I for one have been the subject of such manipulation. Whether it be Netflix or my favourite social media apps, I find myself mindlessly scrolling through posts trying to get my quick fix of distraction and supposed stress relief. However, these feelings don't bring me joy, rather it brings me anxiety that I have wasted precious time and I end up kicking myself for it afterwards. This happens time and time again and it felt like I was stuck in a loop, unable to get out.

So, what is the solution to this seemingly endless spiral of bad habits? Some might say just to delete the apps or turn off Wi-Fi. But how many of you might have actually tried that yourself only to have it backfire on you? Redownloading the app is only one step away, Wi-Fi is only one button away, and addictions aren't so easily kicked to the curb as one might think.

What I have found that works is that instead of consuming mindless media that don't bring about actual benefit to my life, I chose to watch content that I could actually learn something from. Like this channel for example. I went on the hunt to seek out content that I could learn how to make extra money, how to improve my health, how to improve my relationships, basically anything that had to do with personal development. And I found that I actually felt less guilty watching or reading these posts even though they still do take up my time to consume.

You may call it a lesser of two evils, but what I discovered was that it provided much more benefit to my life than actually not consuming any personal development media at all. Whether it be inspirational stories from successful entrepreneurs like Elon Musk, or Jeff Bezos, or multi-billion-dollar investment advice from Warren Buffet, these passive watching of useful content actually boosted my knowledge in areas that I might otherwise have not been exposed to. Subconsciously, i started internalizing some of these beliefs and adopted it into my own psyche. And i transformed what was mindless binge watching of useless Tv shows and zombie content, to something that actually moved the needle in my life in the right direction, even by a little.

Overtime, I actually required less and less distraction of media consumption using my technology devices like iPhones and iPads or Macs and started putting more attention and effort to do the work that I knew i had to get done. Because some of these personal development videos actually taught me what I needed to do to get stuff done and to stop procrastinating in working towards my goals.

So I challenge each and every one of you today to do a thorough review of the kinds of music and media consumption that you consume today with your smartphones and tablets, and see if you can substitute them with something that you can learn from, no matter how trivial you think it may be. It could be the very push you need to start porting over all your bad habits of technology into something that can pay off for you 10 years down the road.

Chapter 19:

Creating Successful Habits

Successful people have successful habits.
If you're stuck in life, feeling like you're not going anywhere, take a hard look at your habits.
Success is built from our small daily habits accumulated together,
Without these building blocks, you will not get far in life.
Precise time management, attention to detail, these are the traits of all who have made it big.
To change your life, you must literally change your life, the physical actions and the mindset.

Just as with success, the same goes with health.
Do you have the habit of a healthy diet and regular athletic exercises?
Healthy people have healthy habits.
If you are unhappy about your weight and figure, point the finger at your habits once again.

To become healthy, happy and wealthy, we must first become that person in the mind.
Success is all psychological.
Success has nothing to do with circumstances.
Until we have mastered the habits of our thinking we cannot project this success on the world.

We must first decide clearly who we want to be.

We must decide what our values are.

We must decide what we want to achieve.

Then we must discipline ourselves to take control of our destiny.

Once we know who we are and what we want to do,

Behaving as if it were reality becomes easy.

We must start acting the part.

That is the measure of true faith.

We must act as if we have already succeeded.

As the old saying goes: "fake it UNTIL YOU MAKE IT"

Commit yourself with unwavering faith.

Commit yourself with careful and calculated action.

You will learn the rest along the way

Every habit works towards your success or failure,

No matter how big or how small.

The more you change your approach as you fail, the better your odds become.

Your future life will be the result of your actions today.

It will be positive or negative depending on your actions now.

You will attain free-will over your thoughts and actions.

The more you take control, the happier you will be.

Guard your mind from negativity.
Your mind is your sanctuary.
Ignore the scaremongering.
Treat your mind to pure motivation.

We cannot avoid problems.
Problems are a part of life.
Take control of the situation when it arises.
Have a habit of responding with action rather than fear.

Make a habit of noticing everybody and respecting everybody.
Build positive relationships and discover new ideas.
Be strong and courageous, yet gentle and reasonable.
These are the habits of successful leaders.

Be meticulous.
Be precise.
Be focused.

Make your bed in the morning.
Follow the path of drill sergeants in the royal marines and US navy seals.
Simple yet effective,
This one habit will shift your mindset first thing as you greet the new day.

Choose to meditate.

Find a comfortable place to get in touch with your inner self.

Make it a habit to give yourself clarity of the mind and spirit.

Visualize your goals and make them a reality in your mind.

Choose to work in a state of flow.

Be full immersed in your work rather than be distracted.

To be productive we need to have an incredible habit of staying focused.

It will pay off.

It will pay dividends.

The results will be phenomenal.

Every single thing you choose to make a habit will add up.

No matter how big or how small,

Choose wisely.

Choose the habit of treating others with respect.

Treat the cleaner the same as you would with investors and directors.

Treat the poor the same as you would with the CEO of a multi-national company.

Our habits and attitude towards ourselves and others make up our character.

Choose a habit of co-operation over competition,

After all the only true competition is with ourselves.

It doesn't matter whether someone is doing better than us as long as we are getting better.
If someone is doing better, we should learn from them.
Make it a habit of putting ourselves into someone else's shoes.
We might stand to learn a thing or two.

No habit is too big or too small.
To be happy and successful we must do our best in them all.

Chapter 20:

Consistency

Today we're going to talk about a very important topic that I believe is one of the core principles that we should all strive to integrate into our lives. And that is consistency.

What does consistency mean to you when you hear that word? For me previously when I kept hearing people say that I would need to stay consistent in this and that, it did not ring any bells in me and i brushed it off thinking it was just another productivity word similar to work hard, be positive and so on. However it was only when I start doing more digging that I realized that many successful people in life actually attributed consistency as being the key factor that led to their success. That it was that one quality they possessed in their work ethic that allowed them to surpass their competition. That they had set out a plan and stuck to it consistency over days, months, years, and even decades until they finally achieved their goals.

You see for many of us, consistency is something that i believe we all struggle with. Whether it be going to the gym, putting in the effort to work out, going for trainings, health wise or work related, studying, practicing an instrument, especially things we find to be not so enjoyable to do, we just do not show up consistently enough to produce results that are satisfactory let alone ones that we are proud of. And we complain that our body doesn't look good, that we are getting nowhere with learning a new instrument, or maybe that we have plateaued in the area that we most wish to desire to move forward in, work or play.

You see, your level of consistency is directly correlated with the amount of time you actually spend on an activity. And if your consistency drops, it is no wonder that your performance drops as well as you are not putting in the adequate amount of time to actually progress forward. As the saying goes, practice makes perfect. And Practice takes time. And time requires consistency.

Highly successful figures in any field, be it sports or the business world, from roger Federer, Lionel Messi, Michael jordan, Kobe Bryant, to Elon Musk, Bill Gates, Steve Jobs, they possess a strong vision for themselves and their consistency is a tool for their success. They would not hesitate to put every ounce of their time and energy into being the best in their field by showing up every single day for practice or for work, to get better each day and to crush their opinion. What they lack in skill, they make up for in consistency in practice. And they improve much faster than their opponents as a result, keeping them at the very top level of their game.

With the knowledge that consistency was the key to success for many entrepreneurs and businessmen, i decided to try it out for myself. Previously I was erratic in my work schedule. I always wandered around my tasks and never put in the effort to put in a set number of hours every day. I felt that my body wasn't getting any fitter, my tennis was average at best, and my income never really went anywhere. In all areas of my life, it felt like i had reached a ceiling.

After making the change to becoming more consistent in everything that I did, I saw a marked improvement in all areas that I had struggled with previously. My body started taking shape, my tennis game improved, and my income grew as well. The thing is, i hadn't done anything different apart from making it a daily habit and routine of putting in more hours into each task, showing up for more gym sessions, showing up for more tennis games, showing up for more hours at work, and consistently putting out more content. While gradual, these hours slowly added up and I saw a breakthrough. And I was surprised at how one small little change in how I approached life actually benefited me. I felt happier that i was improving in all these areas, and it had a snowball effect of actually compounding over time. Sooner or later i was beating my peers in all areas that I was once level with.

I challenge each and everyone of you to make consistency one of your core philosophies in life. To approach each and every task, project, or mission you embark on with a level of consistency unmatched by those around you. I am sure you will be very surprised at what you can achieve with just this one simple tweak in everything that you do.

Chapter 21:

Block Out The Critics and Detractors

There is drama everywhere around us. In fact, our whole life is a drama. A drama that has more complex turns and thrillers than the best thriller ever to be made on a cinema screen.

This drama isn't always a result of our own actions. Sometimes we do something stupid to contribute towards anarchy. But mostly the things happening around us seem to be a drama because the critics make a hell out of everything.

We get sucked into things that and someone else's opinions because we do not know what we are doing.

It may sound cliche but remember that it doesn't matter what anyone else says. In fact, most discoveries and inventions got bad press when they were found or made. It was only after they are gone when people actually came to appreciate the true importance of those inventions.

The time will come sooner or later when you are finally appreciated for your work and your effort. But your work should not depend on what others will say.

Your work should not depend on the hope of appreciation or the fear of criticism, rather it should be done because it was meant to be done. You should put your heart and soul in it because you had a reason for all this and only you will reap the fruit, no matter what the world gets from it.

You don't need to do the best out there in the world and neither should you be judged on that standard. But you should put out the best YOU can do because that will someday shut out the critics as they start to see your true potential.

The work itself doesn't matter, but the effort you put behind it does. You don't need to be an insult to anyone who mocks you or criticizes you on even your best work. Empathy is your best approach to bullying.

You cannot possibly shut out every critic. You spend your whole life trying to answer to those meaningless least important people that weren't even able to make their own lives better. Because those who did make something of themselves didn't find it worthwhile to distract and degrade everyone else.

So you should try to spend your time more and more on your good work. Keep a straight sight without even thinking to look at one more ordinary critic who doesn't give a simple feeling of empathy towards your efforts.

You only need to put yourself in others' shoes and look at yourself through their eyes. If you can do that before them, you would have the best reply to any hurtful comment. And that my friend will be true silence.

People always come to gather around you when they see a cause they can relate to. So give them a cause. Give a ray of hope and motivation to people around you and you will finally get to get the critics on your side.

Your critics will help you get to the top from the hardest side there is.

Chapter 22:

Start Each Day Stress-Free

Getting up in the morning with a blank mind, not knowing what to do. Trying to figure out how to cope with what happened yesterday. We all go through this, right?

But today is an important day and you aren't prepared for it. It stresses us out. It's the first thing we do in the morning, without realizing the impact it'll have on our day.

The entire day will be tainted with negative vibes and worries if you are stressed out in the morning. Your brain will accept that nothing will go right, and you will not be able to accomplish anything. And so, you quit. We stress over things without even trying. You cannot control your source of stress, but you can manage the tension that is making you feel stressed.

Let us take an example. How heavy is a glass of water? About 10-12 ounces. Then if you hold this glass of water for a minute, you will not feel any harm, but in an hour, you will feel pain in your arm, in two hours, your arm will go numb, and in a day, your arm might paralyze. It wasn't the weight of the glass, but how long you held it.

The stress is like this glass. No matter how big or how small the stress is, the longer you hold onto it, the more damage it causes.

Therefore, it is important to start each day stress-free to feel optimism, good vibes, and happiness the whole day. I will tell you how you can start each day unstressed and full of motivation. The first thing you need to do is make sure you sleep well. Even if you are fully prepared, you will end up stressed out if you don't get enough sleep.

Make a to-do list of things you need to do tomorrow, so you wake up every morning knowing what are your today's priorities. Prepare yourself for the next day's activities the night before. Let us say you have an important meeting, set an early alarm, prepare your presentation, keep all your important notes and files on your desk, decide what to wear, etc. Stay calm and know you can handle it. This way you will feel less stressed on your important day.

Suppose you have less than 30 minutes left for an important exam. There are a few questions left. You start stressing about finishing it. You know the answers, but you are worried about time. This stress will trigger the body's "flight or fight" response. You will start sweating, your heart will start beating quickly, your brain will stop responding. Finally you will decide to skip it and rely on what you have already done.

This is what stress does to you, even if you are well prepared for everything. In contrast, if you have remained calm and believed you can do it, you will for sure have completed your test earlier and much more efficiently than you would have otherwise.

Keep in mind that stress doesn't ease your pain or lighten your burden; it just makes things worse. Motivate yourself to achieve today's goal by starting the day with positive energy. It is very important for you to be happy and stress-free in the morning to stay calm and relaxed throughout the day. Try meditation, yoga, morning walk, or whatever makes you stress-free at the start of the day. Don't be so hard on yourself, have confidence and faith in yourself.

Chapter 23:

Stop Hitting That Snooze Button

Life is about the things you can take control of. You live your life day by day. So, every day in your life is a small part that starts with you waking up and ends with you going back to bed. You sleep every night after setting up at least five different alarms. Why do you set all these alarms and then sleep until the last? It is simple; You set these alarms because there have been tasks on your mind that you must do.

You set more than one alarm because you know you will snooze them all for sure. You can't get up on the first alarm because you are too lazy, and you don't have any discipline in your life. Your alarm keeps buzzing, and you wait till the last ring to either snooze it or for it to end. But this is your deciding moment. This is your time to decide if you want to get up or keep snoozing as you have been avoiding and snoozing opportunities your whole life.

This is a battle with yourself to test if you will hit the snooze or if you will get up and do what is necessary. You set alarms to help you get up when the natural causes are not enough. You might be a deep sleeper or a light sleeper, but you need some aid or reminder to get up in the morning. But when you hit that snooze button, you have essentially broken the determination with which you set that alarm last night.

Maybe this was your last chance to succeed. Perhaps this was your last chance to get out of this state of depression and laziness. You aren't probably the guy who promotes success on one's own actions. You can't even handle an alarm on your phone; how do you plan to take the world's mockery when you fail at other things in your life.

If you train yourself to be subconsciously active even before you hear the first alarm, this means you are well equipped to break your sleep cycles whenever you want. This mirrors your dedication to your work and your control over your own body.

If you don't hit the snooze button and go out to work, it will not matter too much if you fail out there. Why? Because now you started your day with success when you acted against your wishes to sleep a little longer and didn't hit that snooze button. Now you are on a power curve, and you feel good about the following things because now you are hopeful. Because now you know you can bring a change within yourself.

When you didn't hit that snooze button, you showed yourself how much this day means to you and how much of a promising character you are. Life is long enough to hit the snooze some other time, but for now, you need to seize the day as it might never be like this again.

Chapter 24:

7 Crucial Life Skills To Have

Life skills is a term used to describe many of your abilities to deal effectively with everyday problems. Whether it's problem-solving, learning decision-making, or acquiring communication skills, life skills expand your thinking and can be helpful in both your personal and professional endeavors.

Here are some essential life skills that everyone should learn and master, regardless of age, gender, location, or situation.

1. Creativity

Creativity is considered one of the essential life skills you can possess. Creativity helps you better solve problems and allows you to see things from a different perspective. Thinking creatively in your personal life or at work can help you think outside the box, come up with fresh ideas and strategies, and better deal with uncertainty. Other benefits of creativity include:

1. You can express yourself candidly and honestly.
2. Reduce stress and anxiety.
3. Give a sense of purpose.
4. Improving thinking and problem-solving skills.
5. It makes you feel proud and accomplished.

2. Problem-Solving

Another helpful life skill to learn and master is problem-solving. Addressing issues that matter to organizations and individuals puts you in control of your environment. Identifying and fixing the root cause of the problem can bring you great satisfaction and success. As you face and overcome many obstacles in your lifetime, troubleshooting can help you:

1. Tests your ability to analyze information and evaluate situations.
2. Propose new strategies to solve problems.
3. Increase your self-esteem and ability level.

3. Communication

Effective communication is a life skill that will take you far, both personally and professionally. You'll meet people from all walks of life throughout your life, so knowing how to be actively involved can help strengthen relationships, increase productivity, and build trust. Other benefits of communication skills include:

1. Improving Relationships at Work.
2. It helps you stay organized.
3. Boost self-esteem.
4. It enables you to create a successful family.
5. Providing opportunities to participate in community life.

4. Leadership

Understanding the power and value of leadership is an essential lifelong learning skill that can profoundly impact the lives of others. Leaders not only have control, they know how to motivate, inspire, and empower others. To be a successful leader, you need to teach them to see the strengths of others and to believe in their worth. Leadership can benefit all areas of your life by helping you:

1. Strengthening communication skills.
2. Character development.
3. Build trust.

Leadership skills can be acquired through experience and education.

5. Critical Thinking

Learning to think critically is critical to future success. Responsible, productive, and independent thinking can help in all areas of life. Thinking systematically helps improve the way you express your thoughts and ideas. Some of the essential benefits of critical thinking are:

1. It helps you make better decisions.
2. Make you happier.
3. Better relationship.

Make sure your comments are educated and well informed. Critical thinking also transcends cultural norms and is open to those around you, helping you learn and understand other factors that can influence the decisions of others.

6. Self Awareness

Self-awareness refers to recognizing or recognizing emotions, beliefs, behaviours, and motivations, among other traits, including strengths and weaknesses. Self-awareness is an essential life skill because it allows us to understand better who we are, how we feel, and what makes us unique and different from others. By becoming self-aware, you can make lifestyle changes that will help you think more positively. Here are some key benefits of self-awareness:

1. Increased communication.
2. Rich emotional intelligence.
3. Improve your listening and empathy skills.
4. Improving Leadership and Opportunities.

7. Empathy

In addition to being assertive, it is imperative to empathize with the people around you. Understanding the feelings of others and showing compassion and support can help us respond appropriately. Whether hanging out with a loved one or showing interest in someone at work, empathy can build trust and eliminate conflicts with others.

Along with interpersonal and challenging skills, life skills are essential, and we cannot deny it. The impact of learning skills on your life is enormous. There are several life skills. In this article, I have mentioned some essential life skills that must be learned.

Chapter 25:

6 Steps to Identify Your Personal Core Values

Discovering your core values can increase your confidence and make it easier to make decisions because you've identified whether a decision aligns with your values. Knowing your values can also help in choosing a career or knowing whether to change careers. Discovering your values takes some time and self-reflection. In this article, we will discuss the steps you should take to discover your values.

What are Values?

The most basic definition of values is a set of beliefs or opinions that influence how you live your life. They are ideas that are important to you personally characterize who you are as an individual. Values play an important role in shaping how you respond to situations and how you set goals.

Examples of Core Values

Everyone's set of core values is unique and influenced by their life experiences. Psychologists also recognize that it's important to stay conscious of your values throughout your life because they can change as your career and personal life develops. To get a sense of your values, it can be helpful to review a list of core values for ideas.

- Achievement
- Ambition
- Caring
- Charity
- Honesty
- Humor
- Individuality
- Joy
- Kindness
- Knowledge
- Leadership
- Motivation
- Optimism
- Personal development
- Resilience
- Risk-taking
- Safety

Follow the steps below to generate a list of your core values:

1. Write Down Your Values

Review the list of examples of core values above and write down every value that resonates with you. Add any you think of that are not on the list as well. Select the values that most accurately describe your feelings or behaviors.

2. Consider The People You Most Admire

Values are typically personified in people whom we admire and love. Generally, when we admire a quality in others, it's because it's something we value ourselves. Write down six people you admire who are role models or valued connections for you.

For example, you could include a colleague because of their perseverance and dedication. You could include a family member because of their empathy. Try to include people you consider heroes as well. For example, you may admire Martin Luther King, Jr. because of his kindness to others and his commitment to fighting for social justice. Note the values that these six people embody.

3. Consider Your Experiences

To learn about your values, think back to the best and most painful moments in your life. Consider what these experiences reveal about your core values. For example, if you won an award for teaching, it's possible that motivating others and leadership are important values for you. A painful experience may have taught you that empathy and compassion are important to you.

4. Categorize Values Into Related Groups

Now you have a master list of values. Next, review the list and see if you can group the values into categories. For example, you may have written down growth, learning, and personal development. These values are all related and could be placed in one category. Another example is if you selected stability, reliability, and punctuality. These values could all be grouped.

5. Identify The Central Theme

Once you have categorized your values, choose a word that best represents the group. You can leave the other words in the group in parentheses next to the central theme word to give the primary value more context.

6. Choose Your Top Core Values

Rank the top values in order of importance. While people's number of core values can vary, it's typically best to narrow them down to five to 10. If you have more than 10, ask yourself what values are essential to your life. You may want to leave them for a day and come back to them later to see if they truly reflect your core values and if they are in the correct order.

Benefits of Identifying Your Values

There are several reasons why it's beneficial to identify your core values. They include:

- **Finding your purpose:** Knowing your values helps you figure out what you want out of your life.
- **Guiding your behavior:** They help you behave in a way that matches who you want to be.

- **Helping you make decisions:** When you're facing a decision, you can ask yourself what someone who values the things you do would choose.
- **Helping you choose a career:** When you know what matters to you, it's easier to choose the right career path.
- **Increasing your confidence:** Identifying your values brings a sense of safety and stability into your life because you know what you want and what's important to you.

Chapter 26:

6 Steps To Get Out of Your Comfort Zone

The year 2020 and 2021 have made a drastic change in all our lives, which might have its effect forever. The conditions of last year and a half have made a certain lifestyle choice for everyone, without having a say in it for us.

This new lifestyle has been a bit overwhelming for some and some started feeling lucky. Most of us feel comfortable working from home, and taking online classes while others want to have some access to public places like parks and restaurants.

But the pandemic has affected everyone more than once. And now we are all getting used to this relatively new experience of doing everything from home. Getting up every day to the same routine and the same environment sometimes takes us way back on our physical and mental development and creativity.

So one must learn to leave the comfort zone and keep themselves proactive. Here are some ways anyone can become more productive and efficient.

Everyone is always getting ready to change but never changing.

1. Remember your Teenage Self

People often feel nostalgic remembering those days of carelessness when they were kids and so oblivious in that teenage. But, little do they take for inspiration or motivation from those times. When you feel down, or when you don't feel like having the energy for something, just consider your teenage self at that time.

If only you were a teenager now, you won't be feeling lethargic or less motivated. Rather you'd be pushing harder and harder every second to get the job done as quickly as possible. If you could do it back then, you still can! All you need is some perspective and a medium to compare to.

2. Delegate or Mentor Someone

Have you ever needed to have someone who could provide you some guidance or help with a problem that you have had for some time?

I'm sure, you weren't always a self-made man or a woman. Somewhere along the way, there was someone who gave you the golden quote that changed you consciously or subconsciously.

Now is the time for you to do the same for someone else. You could be a teacher, a speaker, or even a mentor who doesn't have any favors to ask in return. Once you get the real taste of soothing someone else's pain, you won't hesitate the next time.

This feeling of righteousness creates a chain reaction that always pushes you to get up and do good for anyone who could need you.

3. Volunteer in Groups

The work of volunteering may seem pointless or philanthropic. But the purpose for you to do it should be the respect that you might get, but the stride to get up on your feet and help others to be better off.

Volunteering for flood victims, earthquake affectees or the starving people of deserts and alpines can help you understand the better purpose of your existence. This keeps the engine of life running.

4. Try New Things for a Change

Remember the time in Pre-school when your teachers got you to try drawing, singing, acting, sculpting, sketching, and costume parties. Those weren't some childish approach to keep you engaged, but a planned system to get your real talents and skills to come out.

We are never too old to learn something new. Our passions are unlimited just as our dreams are. We only need a push to keep discovering the new horizons of our creative selves.

New things lead to new people who lead to new places which might lead to new possibilities. This is the circle of life and life is ironic enough to rarely repeat the same thing again.

You never know which stone might lead you to a gold mine. So never stop discovering and experiencing because this is what makes us the supreme being.

5. Push Your Physical Limits

This may sound cliched, but it always is the most important point of them all. You can never get out of your comfort zone, till you see the world through the hard glass.

The world is always softer on one side, but the image on the other side is far from reality. You can't expect to get paid equally to the person who works 12 hours a day in a large office of hundreds of employees. Only if you have the luxury of being the boss of the office.

You must push yourself to search for opportunities at every corner. Life has always more and better to offer at each stop, you just have to choose a stop.

6. Face Your Fears Once and For All

People seem to have a list of Dos and Dont's. The latter part is mostly because of a fear or a vacant thought that it might lead to failure for several reasons.

You need a "Do it all" behavior in life to have an optimistic approach to everything that comes in your way.

What is the biggest most horrible thing that can happen if you do any one of these things on your list? You need to have a clear vision of the possible worst outcome.

If you have a clear image of what you might lose, now must try to go for that thing and remove your fear once and for all. Unless you have something as important as your life to lose, you have nothing to fear from anything.

No one can force you to directly go skydiving if you are scared of heights. But you can start with baby steps, and then, maybe, later on in life you dare to take a leap of faith.

"Life is a rainbow, you might like one color and hate the other. But that doesn't make it ugly, only less tempting".

All you need is to be patient and content with what you have today, here, right now. But, you should never stop aiming for more. And you certainly shouldn't regret it if you can't have or don't have it now.

People try to find their week spots and frown upon those moments of hard luck. What they don't realize is, that the time they wasted crying for what is in the past, could have been well spent for a far better future they could cherish for generations to come.

Chapter 27:

Schedule Your Motivation

Motivation does not appear magically, nor do you stay motivated all the time. This is the main reason you fail; you get motivated at times by some inspirational stories or
Debates or quotes, but mostly you fail to maintain that motivation.

At the moment, you make vague plans but are not able to implement them. So how can you stay motivated and accomplish your goals?

What do you think about how successful people remain motivated all the time? This is because they schedule their motivation, set their aims, manifest them day by day, week by week, and stick to it till they finally achieve them.

The most crucial part of achieving your goals is planning your motivation. Scheduling is not a prison, rather it is the way you will live your day based on what is important to you so that it is productive. If you do not schedule your motivation and wait for the willpower to wake you up this is what causes your failure.

You need to pre-plan to decide what and when you want to work on, but starting work without a schedule will waste half of your capacity and time on deciding when, where, and how to begin, which will leave you demotivated and failed.

Maintaining a healthy balance between work and personal life is another important reason why you should schedule your motivation. The continuous grind of work, staying away from loved ones, giving up on all physical or outdoor activities not only affect your mental health but also leave you with misery and suffering.

Everyone has a strict timetable. Everyone has a daily regime of actions and duties that they need to do to keep the wheel turning. But when do we have the time to take a moment off and motivate ourselves to continue doing the good work.

You need to take some time off to pat yourself on the back to acknowledge and appreciate what you have done till now is good. But at the same time, you also need to push yourself to do better.

Whatever you are doing is good and better in the first place, that is why you are getting good results. But you need to ask yourself, Can I do better?

If you have even the smallest belief in your efforts, your potential, your talents; you will naturally try to work even harder and your skills will sharpen with each second.

You might ask, Why would I need to get better? The answer to that is that if you don't keep up with the pace of this world, you are meant to be left behind by someone else sooner or later.

You don't prioritize the things on your schedule, you only need to schedule the things that you prioritize. Because that is the only way you can work up to new, more and better things.

You will eventually get to a state where you are perfect at that one thing, and then, you will find more things to perfect.

Chapter 28:

5 Ways To Focus on Creating Positive Actions

Only a positive person can lead a healthy life. Imagine waking up every day feeling like you are ready to face the day's challenges and you are filled with hope about life. That is something an optimist doesn't have to imagine because they already feel it every day. Also, scientifically, it is proven that optimistic people have a lower chance of dying because of a stress-caused disease. Although positive thinking will not magically vanish all your problems, it will make them seem more manageable and somewhat not a big deal.

All you have to do is focus on the positive side of life. It is not necessarily true that people with a positive mindset always get disappointed. Positivity is like a breath of fresh air for us. Looking at the bright side of things has its advantages, and it has its very own benefits. So, positive energy is an essential factor to produce in oneself to make them more efficient in the ways of life. They tend to focus on all the good things and push aside all the wrong things, making them love everything they do.

1. Think Positively

Positive thinking is what leads to positive actions, actions that affect you and the people around you. When you think positively, your actions show how positive you are. You can create positive thinking by focusing on the good in life, even if it may feel tiny thing to feel happy about because when you once learn to be satisfied with minor things, you would think that you no longer feel the same amount of stress as before and now you would feel freer. This positive attitude will always find the good in everything, and life would seem much easier than before. You then become the person you once imagined yourself to be, just by thinking positively about it. So, make sure to process those positive thoughts thoroughly for better results or action.

2. Be Grateful

Being grateful for the things you have contributed a lot to your positive behavior. Gratitude has proven to reduce stress and improve self-esteem. Think of the things you are grateful for; for example, if someone gives you good advice, then be thankful to them, for if someone has helped you with something, then be grateful to them, by being grateful about minor things, you feel more optimistic about life, you feel that good things have always been coming to you. Studies show that making down a list of things you are grateful for during hard days helps you survive tough times. Also, be thankful to yourself for making achievements that you wanted. It makes you feel positive about yourself and makes your confidence boost through you. You have to make sure that you know what it is to be thankful for. Be grateful to someone for all the right reasons, and you will feel positive.

3. Laugh Through Situations

A person laughing always looks like a happy person. Studies have shown that laughter lowers stress, anxiety, and depression. Open yourself up to humor, permit yourself to laugh even if forced because even a forced laugh can improve your mood. Laughter lightens the mood and makes problems seem more manageable. Your laughter is contagious, and it may even enhance the perspective of the people around us. Smiling is free therapy. You have to pass an approving smile and make someone's day up.

4. Don't Blame Yourself For The Things You Can't Control

People with depression or anxiety are always their jailers; being harsh on themselves will only cause pain, negativity, and insecurity. So try to be soft with yourself, give yourself a positive talk regularly; it has proven to affect a person's actions. A positive word to yourself can influence your ability to regulate your feelings and thoughts. The positivity you carry in your brain is expressed through your actions, and who doesn't loves an optimistic person. Instead of blaming yourself, you can think differently, like "I will do better next time" or "I can fix this." Being optimistic about the complicated situation can lead your brain to find a solution to that problem.

5. Start Your Day with A dose of Positivity

When you wake up, it is good to do something positive in the morning, which mentally freshens you. You can start the day by reading a positive quote about life and understand the meaning of that quote, and you may feel an overwhelming feeling after letting the meaning set. Everybody loves a good song, so start by listening to a piece of music that gives you positive vibes, that gives you hope, and motivation for the day. You can also share your positivity by being nice to someone or doing something nice for someone; you will find that you feel thrilled and positive by making someone else happy.

Conclusion

Indeed, we can not just start thinking positively overnight, but we have to push ourselves more every time to improve. Surround yourself with brightness, good people, and a positive mindset—a good combination for a good life.

Chapter 29:

Five Ways To Be Inspired

Inspiration

What really is inspiration? It is what pushes you to go the extra mile. Inspiration is what fuel is to a motor vehicle. It powers it to continue with the journey.

You are never late to be inspired. Every moment is a time for inspiration. At any one point in our lives, we need to be inspired to do more. Sometimes are demotivated by the outcomes of life when we do not get what we had hoped for. That is not the time to throw in the towel.

All you need to do is look in the right direction. You need a second voice to encourage you and pat you on the shoulder.

An inspired person is transformed and renewed in their thoughts. It is like they dropped from the skies because all they think of is how they shall beat that target or how they will turn around their fortunes.

Not many people in this generation are inspired to move towards their goals. Here are five ways to be inspired:

1. Reflect On Your Achievements

Your life could have reached a plateau phase, at least in your eyes. You may lack the motivation to move ahead with your plans because everything seems to be pre-determined. The good news is that a plateau is better than level ground.

Turn your head and look at the far that you have come from. You overcame what others did not. Now is not the time to give up.

Think of the promise you gave your loved ones and consider how far your hard work has brought you. Imagine the smiles and laughter on their faces when you finally make it.

That is the spirit! Keep pushing!

2. Focus On Your Goals, Not Problems

The end goal of your journey is what you should focus on, never on your problems.

Consider the example of a lion chasing its prey. When he chooses a particular antelope from a herd, there is no turning back. He will keep chasing it until he wins. It does not matter whether another animal will pass in front of him. He will not lose focus on the one he had selected.

Victory tastes sweet. You should not think about anything that will make you miss it. Nothing is worth missing the prize.

There is a reason why you set out on the path you have chosen. Stick to whatever inspired you in the first place.

3. Have A Mentor

Do you have someone whom you idolize? There is this person who is all you would want to be. You would give everything in exchange to be him/her. Their dressing, their work ethic, and all their personal lifestyle reflect your desires and ambitions.

Mentors are people who inspire you not to be average. Whenever you are at the brink of giving up, their level of success cannot give you peace.

Your inspiration shoots above the roof when you spend time with them. Use your time with them to learn about their journey and how they overcame the challenges they faced.

Most important is that the success and failures of your mentor will make you realize they are also human but they managed to overcome it all.

You too can make it!

4. Build Your Self-Confidence

The reason why some people are demotivated is because of low self-confidence. They do not believe in themselves. They hand their competitors any slight opportunity on a platter. They suffer from an inferiority complex.

Build your personality. Train, read, and research. Do what it takes to give you confidence in your ability. Do not be timid for any reason.

Do not be your own enemy. When experts are being called forward and you are one of them, proudly move forward. What you despise in you is the dream of many people out there.

5. Stay Updated

It is important to be up to date with the latest trends in your field of interest. Do not lag behind because you will not feel the need to catch up.

There is an inspiration to catch up with the latest developments. The more you follow closely, the more you want to keep up. This is enough motivation.

These five ways will inspire you to get out of your comfort zone. It is what you really need in the wake of stiff competition everywhere.

Chapter 30:

How You're Demotivated by Burnout

We have this problem in our lives when we try to deal with too many things simultaneously. We constantly juggle so many things and try to balance everything. But the truth is, not everything is the same, nor should it be dealt with equally.

We often come to realize it on our own. But we do not come across it on smooth corners when we do. The harshest endings or lessons often teach us what was essential and what was not.

This is when we can't look beyond what we lost, and this is when we feel like a failure!

The thing is, we have a lot on our plate, but we cannot distinguish between the most important of these things. We prioritize everything equally, and this is when failure hits us the hardest. Humans are very much capable of handling a lot of things simultaneously but are not able to deal with multiple failures as well!

We all are bound to fail at one point or another in our lives, but how we bounce back is what matters.

Burnout is a risk that too many of us take, and you should be well aware that your work life is something you can drop and pick up whenever you want. But there is also your family, your health, your friends that you are taking for granted and trying to make all things work out simultaneously.

But this is too much for anyone, and you are not ready for this. Maybe you never will, and perhaps you are not meant to be able to juggle between all these things.

This is why you cannot find the proper motivation, and this is why you cannot find the right path to success. You cannot find the right track because you are making the wrong one for yourself. The wrong course is always trying too hard to focus on one thing for some time and give all the other things what they deserve.

Everything and everyone in your life needs your utmost attention, just not always for everything at the same time.

You need to take some time off and talk with yourself. You don't always need to outperform yourself. Pushing your limits is good, but this pushing should also be put to a limit.

Pushing your boundaries is good but breaking yourself in that process isn't. How do you know that you are close to burnout is if everything starts to feel like a burden or when even your breathing seems to be labored. You start feeling frustrated at little things, and this is when you dive into depression and lose motivation.

I get it; you need to provide for the people around you. But you also need to make sure that you don't hurt yourself in the long run.
You should not burn yourself to keep others warm. You only need to renew the fire you started. The fire doesn't require you to jump in it; it just needs you to keep feeding it the fuel.

Chapter 31:

3 Ways To Master Your Next Move

"I don't know what to do with my life!" If you find yourself saying this, you're not alone. It's common for people to get to a point where they feel stuck or directionless. It can result from poor decision making or an inability to make decisions at all.

This state of not knowing what to do next applies to a lot of people, at any age and at different times in your life.

Personally, I have discovered that following these 5 steps will help you to find out what to do with your life, feel good, and get unstuck.

1. Get Moving and Clear Your Mind

"Not knowing what you want is a lot better than knowing exactly what you want but not being able to get it, at least you have hope."

I once faced a very challenging and emotional time; all I could do was think about what I needed to do to get to the next day.

There were no thoughts of what I wanted to do in the future nor were there any thoughts of how I wanted my life to be. It was just a matter of surviving from one day to the next.

For me, during this challenging time, when I was telling myself, "I don't know what to do with my life," exercise was the solution to helping me get through my day.

Every morning my alarm would go off at 6 am. I would have my running gear ready by the bed. I would get dressed, walk out the door, and start running for 45 minutes.

For a long time, it was hard to get out of bed and go for my run because I just wanted to hide away. Over time, I began to look forward to my morning run as I felt more energized, and I was sleeping better.

2. Wake Your Conscious Mind and Limit Choices

"Nobody is going to do your life for you. You have to do it yourself, whether you're rich or poor, out of money or making it, the beneficiary of ridiculous fortune or terrible injustice…Self-pity is a dead end road. You can make the choice to drive down it. It's up to you to decide to stay parked there or to turn around and drive out." -Cheryl Stryed.

Life isn't predictable, and the solutions we seek to answer our life questions don't always come nicely wrapped. There are no rules to follow, and you have to work hard to define your life pathway when you don't know what to do with your life.

Waking our conscious minds to accept our reality and embrace change is one step toward finding out what we need to do next in our life.

We become paralyzed rather than liberated by the power of choice. When we are presented with too many options, our brain doesn't know what to do with it all.

Research has shown that there is a sweet spot when it comes to choices. If we have too few, we feel limited. If we have too many, we feel overwhelmed.

How does this translate to your everyday life? If you're changing career fields and aren't sure what to switch over to, limit your options to five or six possible areas. Choose to mark one off the list every few days once you've sat with the choices a bit. As your brain focuses on fewer and fewer choices, it will become easier to see the direction you genuinely want to go in.

3. Take Small Steps With a 30-Day Challenge

In order to reprogram your conscious mind and stop saying "I don't know what to do with my life," set yourself a 30-day challenge.

You may ask, why 30 days? Because this is how the small steps you take gradually become your powerful habits

Setting a deadline has a powerful effect on motivation. Research has shown time and again that deadlines, even those that are self-imposed, can reduce procrastination and lead to better decision making.

Try setting one to three goals to be achieved during your 30-day challenge. Maybe you want to learn to code. Set weekly goals related to free online courses, and by the end of the month you'll have a good deal of knowledge under your belt.

Or perhaps you want to spend more time with your kids. Make a goal to have one family night each week where you offer all of your attention to your kids. You can even let them help plan what you will do on that special night.

Achieving these goals after one month will give you the confidence and self belief to keep going. It also helps you avoid doing nothing while you're feeling stuck. Once you know you can achieve one goal, you'll go on to achieve more and more.

www.ingramcontent.com/pod-product-compliance
Lightning Source LLC
Chambersburg PA
CBHW072102110526
44590CB00018B/3276